MW00939626

Julie's Story,

Julie Miller, MSW

AuthorHouse™
1663 Liberty Drive, Suite 200
Bloomington, IN 47403
www.authorhouse.com
Phone: 1-800-839-8640

This book is a work of non-fiction. Unless otherwise noted, the author and the publisher make no explicit guarantees as to the accuracy of the information contained in this book and in some

First published by AuthorHouse 10/8/2008

ISBN: 978-1-4389-2276-8 (sc)

Printed in the United States of America
Bloomington, Indiana

This book is printed on acid-free paper.

This book is dedicated to my family: my mom, dad, husband, precious son, sister, and several aunts and family members who have been my loving and caring support throughout my ten-year struggle with lupus.

Contents

CHAPTER 1:

LIVING THE DREAM?

It was the fall of 1997. My life was going just as I had planned. Everything was in order. And I liked order; I lived for it. If my family or friends were to describe me, they would say I was one of the most organized, detail-oriented, well-thought-out individuals you'd meet. I was newly engaged to my college sweetheart and working on finishing a master's degree in school social work. I was in the process of planning my wedding I had dreamed of since I was a little girl. I always wanted a May wedding but unfortunately had to plan it for the month of September, 1998, due to the fact that the reception hall was booked during May.

Trying to complete my master's degree in school social work in eighteen months took a great deal of commitment. I was so grateful to have my mom there to help me plan my wedding. My fiancé, Mike, was busy working on his bachelor's degree in business at a home mortgage institution, as well as working part-time teaching swimming lessons to children. His goal was to save money for us to buy a house after we married. We were both young, eager, twenty-three-year-old adults ready to take on the world, so proud of our achievements we worked so hard for.

The next few months to follow were exciting, yet demanding. I found myself lacking energy and overly fatigued—not unusual for an individual who is planning a wedding for two hundred guests, writing papers, going to classes, having an internship, and studying diligently around the clock. Thankfully, my mom and dad supported me financially, and I was still living at home with them. I prayed that my marriage to Mike would be the loving, devoted marriage my parents have had. After thirty-eight years of marriage, they had to be doing something right.

My mom and I went to lunch after a long day of shopping for wedding dresses. "So what's your secret, Mom?" I asked her, looking for just the right answer.

"Secret to what?" she questioned.

"Secret to having such a great marriage to Dad. I mean, I have never seen the two of you fight, and you always get along so well."

"Admit when you're wrong," she replied.

"What? That's it? You know I can't do that. I'm never wrong!" I said with a chuckle.

"Oh, boy, I see trouble in paradise already." Mom laughed. "You and Mike will be just fine. You get along so well and have been together for six years already. Just remember to keep a sense of humor and don't take things too seriously. Keep God in your relationship and everything will work out." Mom finished the advice on a serious note. I thanked her and have kept that advice in my heart to this day.

Although I can barely remember having the flu, much less the sniffles, as a child, I did suffer with mild headaches when I was young, which eventually became migraines during my teen years. I was put on prescription medication, called Midrin, at the age of twenty-four, which helped the migraines subside. However, by September 1997, I began suffering from excruciating migraines. The pain was so extreme I did not even know what to do with myself. I tried ice packs, showers, and lying down in a dark room, but nothing but time would take the pain away. Sometimes these migraines would last up to twenty-four hours and I would literally get sick from the pain. I again attributed this all to the stresses of my present life situations. Unfortunately, I missed many days of classes and my internship due to these horrific, unpredictable attacks. Thankfully, I had understanding professors and supervisors, who allowed me to make up the hours on my own time. Missing classes was difficult for me to deal with, considering that all through my school years, I strived for perfect attendance, which I achieved for many years.

One day, as I was going to one of my college classes, I remember walking up the stairs and becoming extremely short of breath. My first thought, believe it or not, was that I was extremely out of shape and I really needed to start exercising. *I really haven't had much time to work out due to the fact that I have just been sitting around most of the time studying, typing papers, and counseling students at my internship, where I sit.* No wonder I was so out of shape. Not to mention, my eating habits were not so healthy. I would grab fast food on the run when I had the chance due to my busy schedule (when I had an appetite, that is). Therefore, I thought I would begin to walk on the treadmill thirty minutes every night before bed. *This should help*, I thought to myself.

Despite my few setbacks, which I tried not to mention to my mom (she is quite the worrier), my mom and I were still having fun planning the wedding. Mike and I decided on a beautiful wine-and-pearl-colored angel theme for the September 12th, 1998 wedding. My mom was already helping in planning my wedding shower by looking for angel decorations. I was beginning to really get used to the idea of a September wedding even though my original plan was to have the wedding May 16th.

The exercise I put into place really didn't seem to help with my shortness of breath much. As a matter of fact, it didn't help at all. If anything, the problem became increasingly worse. I could barely walk the treadmill for five minutes. What was I thinking? I found myself taking the elevator over the stairs at school even if I only had to go up one floor. This I kept quiet to everyone I knew. I had no idea what was causing this symptom. After all, I looked perfectly healthy on the outside. I didn't think anyone would believe me that I was having a problem with shortness of breath. I was way too young!

I decided to do my own research on my health problems. On my own time, I went to the public library to investigate my symptoms. All of my problems led me to one conclusion: I had Angina, a temporary chest pain or sensation of pressure that occurs when the heart muscle isn't receiving enough oxygen. At least this is what *I* thought I had. For sure the symptoms matched the diagnosis perfectly. My grandma had heart disease, and although she was in her eighties, I figured it must be hereditary. I was not going to tell anyone; of course they would be worried. Research reports said I would be dying soon.

As the months became colder, a new symptom appeared. As I was walking to my car from class one cold day in December 1997, I noticed that I had no feeling in the tips of my fingers. Although I had gloves on and hadn't walked very far, my fingers were completely numb. I got to my car and took my gloves off. I was shocked at what I saw! The tips of my fingers were ghostly white. I had lost all circulation. I panicked for a moment because I had never had this happen before. I immediately turned on the heat in my car and put my hand up to the vent. A few minutes later, my fingers were normal again. I then figured I needed to buy warmer gloves. Little did I know what was really going on inside my body. All of these symptoms my body was presenting were telling me that something serious was happening. Yet I did not know the real truth.

As the winter months dragged on, I struggled to keep up with my internship, which was the most difficult thing I endured. Many times I would have to leave early due to my intense migraines. I say this was the most difficult because my internship was a forty-five-minute drive one way. I had to intern three days a week. Driving with a migraine is horrible. I remember pulling my car over on the expressway on several occasions because I did not want to get sick in my car. I didn't dare mention this to anyone because I knew how much my family worried. As a matter of fact, my mom worries so much that it literally makes *her* sick.

As March rolled on, I thankfully came to the end of my internship. I did enjoy counseling young children. However, I'm sure I would have liked it so much more if my physical health did not interfere. Classes were also winding down and exams were on the way. Graduation was just a month away, and the wedding was six months away. I tried so hard to hide the pain or at least ignore what was going on within me. I didn't want to believe anything more than stress, anxiety, or pressure was causing such great pain. The shortness of breath became worse. At this point, when I was with my mom or a friend, I recall having to make an excuse to stop walking just to catch my breath.

It was April. Finally, I had made it. Classes were over, my internship was complete, and graduation was a week away. My mom and I went to my cousin Katy's softball tournament on a sunny yet cool day, to relax and cheer her on. After a few hours of sitting in the sun, my mom said, "Julie, you look as though you may have a sunburn on your face."

"That's silly," I replied. "It's April. How can I get a sunburn in April? This is Michigan!" Later that evening, when I looked in the mirror, my face looked as though it had broken out in a terrible red rash on my cheeks, nose, and forehead. *Yes, I guess I should have worn sunscreen.* I called my mom, a bit concerned. "I'm surprised nobody else got burned," I said.

I was so glad to get home from the tournament that day so I could just lie down. I was so sick on that day and wanted so bad to speak of my pain to my parents. No matter how old I get, it makes me feel better to have my mom there when I'm sick. It just seemed difficult to explain exactly what I was going through because every inch of my body was engulfed with such agonizing pain that no one could relate to my suffering. How could I describe to my family that I hurt everywhere even though, except for a little rash, I looked fine on the outside? I remember trying to tell my fiancé, Mike, of my pains. I will never forget his reaction: "Are you sure it's not all in your head?" I don't think his intentions were to be insensitive, but I also don't think he wanted to believe that anything could possibly be wrong with me.

My mom knew I did not feel well on this day; however, she did not know the severity of it. I remember her saying as a joke, "Just don't get sick to the point where you need medical attention, because now that you are not in school anymore, you are no longer under our health insurance. And you don't have a job yet."

I laughed and said, "Oh, wouldn't that be horrible timing!" Little did we know at that time how true this conversation would end up being.

It was graduation day. I had used a whole bottle of makeup concealer to try to cover up my red rash. I will remember that day so clearly. I was getting my black cap and gown on. As I was getting dressed, I remember looking down at my stomach. I could not see my own feet. My stomach protruded out so far it was scary. I stepped on the scale. My normal five-foot-seven-inch, one-hundred-and-ten-pound frame was now up to one hundred and forty-five pounds! I had gained thirty-five pounds in only two weeks. (Strange, because I had had no appetite for the past two months). I suddenly got a horrible cramp in my side, which would not subside. *What is going on!* I cried to myself. Just when things were coming together, they were falling apart. I did the only thing left I could do: *pray.* "God, just get me through this day; that is all I ask. I've worked too hard and come too far. Amen." I was able to get up, finish getting ready, and put a genuine smile on my face for the day.

I got through the graduation ceremony, barely. I wish I could have enjoyed it more. The family had a celebration for me and congratulated me on my accomplishments. I wanted to tell everyone how much pain I was in. Especially Mike and my parents. But this was supposed to be the greatest day of my life.

I didn't want to spoil it. If I did say something, they might take me to the hospital, and who likes hospitals, after all? I wanted pain relief in the worst way, but at the same time, I was honestly so worried that I may not come out of the hospital. *Do I really look sick?* Aside from a little rash, which actually looked like a mild case of sunburn, I looked pretty good—not bad at all.

CHAPTER 2:

THE DIAGNOSIS

A few days after graduation, Mike and I started our marriage classes, which were required by the Catholic Church. We had to go once a week for six weeks. The first week was very interesting. We learned a lot about each other and our similarities and differences. Mike and I have known each other since 1992. We met in college at Grand Valley State University in Allendale, Michigan. We had that instant connection, became friends, and then decided to take our relationship to the next level. Mike is a very loving, caring individual, who puts his needs before others. I knew he would make a great husband and father. People say a girl tends to marry someone like her father. Mike is very much like my dad. I made sure of it!

The second week of class, as I was slowly making my way up the stairs with Mike's help, the shortness of breath, which I normally would try to ignore, got the best of me. I had to stop halfway up. Mike held my hand and asked me if I needed to go to the emergency room. He knew something was seriously wrong. I told him no, and we went to class.

"Mike, it's time," I said as the class was dismissed.

"Time for what?" Mike asked nervously.

"I need to go to the emergency room *now!*" I demanded. I suddenly felt as though I was having a heart attack. There was tremendous pain in my chest that I never felt before and I couldn't breathe. It was the most frightening experience ever.

I did not know a Pontiac Grand Am could go as fast as it did that evening. Luckily, the hospital was nearby. When we arrived, we noticed a sign saying "If you have chest pain, tell personnel immediately." I told the triage nurse that I was having chest pains and shortness of breath. She took one look at me and said, "Have a seat, honey. We'll be with you shortly."

Thirty-five minutes went by before I was seen. I was taken into a room where my blood pressure was checked: 160 over 110. "Wow, that is a high reading," I acknowledged.

The nurse looked at me and said, "Yes, it may be because you are nervous or had caffeine recently." I did not question her and waited for the doctor to examine me. The doctor came in and put pressure on my chest.

"Does this hurt here?" he asked.

"Yes, right there," I moaned in pain. Two more doctors came in and did the same exam. The result? They diagnosed me with Costochrondritis, meaning inflammation of the chest wall. I was sent home with painkillers and told to rest for the next couple days; no problem there.

For the next two days, I was nauseous, dizzy, and vomiting. This may have been due to the pain medication or the pain itself, I'm not sure. But something was still not right. By this point, my mom was absolutely beside herself. She was so worried that she insisted that I call a regular physician and gave me the phone number (which I have had memorized since that agonizing day).

The next day, I called the number my mom gave me. This number led me to a new doctor, Dr. Robert Lang. Although he was a new, young doctor, this day he possibly made the best decision in his life in saving a patient's life. The day I saw him, I was so sick that I could barely walk into his office. It was May 11th, 1998, at 8:00 a.m.—a beautiful, sunny morning. I walked hunched over because my chest pains were so bad I could not stand up straight. The minute I saw him, he took one look at me and knew something serious was wrong. He performed a series of tests, including blood pressure, urine, and a physical exam. Ten minutes later, he told me that I had significant blood and protein in my urine, which was reason for concern.

Mike was in the waiting room. Dr. Lang called Mike into the room and told him that the best thing would be for him to take me to the hospital immediately as a direct admit. He did not know what was wrong with me. However, he did know that my kidneys were involved and needed attention immediately! The specialists there would have to do many tests to find the diagnosis. "So it's not Costochronditis?" I questioned.

"No, it is much worse," Dr. Lang responded. At this point, I was much too sick and the pain was too intense to be worried or scared. Honestly, I just wanted this pain to go away so I could go on living a normal life again. Little did I know, I would not go on to live a normal life again.

Mike called my mom at work, trying not to sound upset. "Mom, the doctor wants Julie to have some tests done at the hospital. I'm bringing her there now."

Not surprisingly, my mom responded with concern. "What hospital? I'll be right there!"

As we were driving to the hospital, I kept thinking of just going home. "How will I pay for this? I have no insurance. What am I going to do? *I just wanted to turn around and forget the whole thing. Then the unbearable pain reminded me of why I was headed downtown.*

When I arrived at the hospital, a team of doctors were already there, ready to begin testing. I had blood test after blood test, chest X-rays, CAT scans, leg scans, a kidney biopsy, an echocardiogram, ultrasounds, you name it. Thankfully, I was given pain medication, which helped tremendously in easing the horrendous agony I was in when I arrived. At this point, I didn't care what testing was done, as long as the pain was eased. My mom arrived not too long after the first test was completed and was already asking doctors what was wrong with me. They told her more testing had to be done. "Will she need to stay the night here?" my mom asked anxiously.

"We suspect she will need to be here until we find out what is wrong with her. We don't know how long it will be. Yes, she will be here overnight, possibly a few nights," the doctors replied.

"I will go home and bring you back some clothes," my mom told me in a matter-of-fact tone.

It was 2:00 a.m. when I heard the nurse come in to give me more pain medication. She told me that the chest X-ray came back and showed a significant amount of fluid around my heart (pericardial effusion) and lungs (pleurisy), which was causing the shortness of breath and chest pains. *Great,* I thought. *Just get rid of the fluid. I'll be fine and I can go home.* When I woke up later that morning, I heard whispering just outside my hospital room. It was my mom, Mike, and the team of doctors. *Why are they whispering?* I thought to myself. "Mom!" I yelled to her.

"Oh good, you are awake. How are you feeling, honey?" she asked genuinely.

"Not so well, Mom," I replied. "What is everyone talking about?" I questioned.

"Oh, just what tests need to be done. Nothing to worry about," she insisted. Mike later told me that the doctors were actually talking about not knowing what was wrong with me, saying it could be cancer, even Leukemia. They just didn't know yet.

The worst part about being the patient is feeling as though you are being kept in the dark about what is going on. For so long, I kept my family in the dark with my aches and pains, and at that point, I didn't know what was going on with my own body. It was a horrible feeling. "Mom, the hospital bill is going to be huge. What am I going to do?" I asked her.

"That is the last thing you need to worry about. Just concentrate on getting better," she responded.

Days and days of tests. Hours and hours of playing the waiting game and wondering if doctors would ever come up with a diagnosis. My mom was my awesome support during this trying time in the hospital. She took personal days from work to be with me. I remember her always making jokes just so I would laugh to make light of the nerve-racking ordeal. However, I knew what stress and worry she felt, as well. Without her sense of humor, though, I'm not sure I could have made it through. My mom believed in the saying "Laughter is the best medicine." I really believed that helped me out in a big way. One day in the hospital, I remember my mom and I looking out of the room, into the hall, at a huge machine with many tubes attached coming past my room. "Look, Julie, just be glad that machine is not coming in this room for you," my mom chuckled with a smile.

"No kidding!" I strongly agreed. No more than thirty seconds later, the exact machine that had passed my room entered my room. And, yes, it was for me.

A team of doctors swarmed into my room. They all had a very concerned yet relieved look on their faces. The head of the team of doctors spoke up and told me that they finally came up with a diagnosis. I took a deep breath. "Julie, you have systemic lupus erythematosus (SLE) with nephritis. Lupus, for short," the doctor said in a serious tone. I heard the words but thought they were speaking a different language. I had never heard of this before. On one hand, I was relieved because I did not hear the word *cancer, leukemia,* or *angina*. On the other hand, I was scared to death because I had never heard of lupus. I took one look at my mom and I could tell she was ready to drill the doctors with questions. "What is lupus?" I asked immediately. The doctors explained that lupus is an autoimmune disease where the immune system becomes overactive and attacks the body. The disease causes inflammation in many parts of the body, and lupus can affect virtually any internal organ. In my case, my kidneys, lungs, heart, skin, joints, and blood were all affected. (Later, I found out there are actually three types of lupus; systemic; discoid, where only the skin is affected; and drug-induced lupus, where a certain drug may cause lupus symptoms and once the drug is stopped, the lupus will subside.)

Looking back now, it made sense why I was never sick when I was younger. I was thinking that my immune system may have always been overactive to some point, so that every time I had

an invader in my body, my immune system must have killed the
intruder. Now that I was older, my immune system went into
overdrive and wham! *I had Lupus.*

With that in mind, I looked at the machine behind the
doctors and asked, "Is that thing going to cure me?" The
doctors looked at each other and told me there was no cure
for lupus as of yet. The doctors reassured me that the disease
is manageable with treatments and medications. This was one
of the treatments that was going to hopefully help me feel
better. It was a process called plasmapheresis, drawing blood
and removing the immune complexes from the plasma, then
returning healthy cells to the body.

The doctors continued to tell me that I also needed IV
Cytoxan chemotherapy. Chemotherapy is something I had
heard of. This, to me, did not sound good. "Lupus is not a cancer,
so why do I need chemotherapy?" I questioned the doctors.

"This will help get the lupus under control. We need to
suppress your immune system because it is overactive. The
chemo will kill the intruders, the overactive cells in your
body. Ideally, this will put you in a remission, where the lupus
symptoms are silent. A flare, on the other hand, is when the
lupus symptoms are active. Your kidneys are in poor shape.
Your chest cavity is filled with fluid. If you would have waited

23

two or three more days before coming in to the hospital, you could have possibly went into cardiac arrest and died," the doctor said in a straightforward manner. Now I was beginning to truly comprehend the severity of my illness.

Thank God Dr. Lang made the best decision and sent me to the hospital! I thought.

The doctor went on to explain to me that I had almost all eleven symptoms that fit the criteria of lupus, which was surprising, because an individual only has to have four of the eleven criteria present to make a lupus diagnosis. The sunburn that I thought I had was actually called a butterfly rash, triggered by the sun. My cold and numb fingertips were also a sign of lupus called Raynaud's phenomenon. This is a condition in which the blood vessels of the hands (or other areas) go into spasm. The unbearable chest pains were due to the pericarditis, which is an inflammation of the lining of the heart. The difficulty in walking and breathing was due to the inflammation of the lining of the lungs, pleurisy. My kidneys were affected (proteinuria), which is why the excessive protein and blood was found in the urine. My severe joint pain (inflammation), headaches, fatigue, and the blood tests markers for lupus (ANA, anti-DNA, complement levels) were all signs of the impending diagnosis.

Knowing very little about lupus at this point, I began to blame myself, thinking that it may have been something I did—or didn't do, for that matter—that caused me to have gotten this awful disease. After all, up to this point in my life, I wasn't the typical health nut. I reviewed my life. I ate junk food and fast food like normal young adults do, but nothing out of the ordinary. I was an athletic teenager with a normal weight. I didn't drink alcohol, smoke, or do drugs. What in the world could have caused this? I pondered and wanted to find out a reason for this disease so that I could stop this from happening to someone else. Heck, maybe I was being punished for not being the greatest daughter at times or not being so nice to my sister when we were growing up. I was thinking of everything I did wrong in my life to be punished with this disease.

I asked the doctor, "What causes lupus?"

The doctor answered hesitantly, "Lupus is a complex disease, and its cause is unknown. It is likely a combination of genetic, environmental, and possibly hormonal factors that work together to contribute to the disease. It is more common in women than men."

I looked at my mom, who shrugged her shoulders and shook her head in confusion. "I don't know anyone in our family who had an autoimmune disease such as lupus," she replied. "I will further research this," she continued. This calmed my worries in thinking I may have caused my illness. On the other hand, I feared tremendously for my future children's lives.

The doctor began to discuss the side effects of the chemotherapy with me. This was all starting to feel like a bad dream. All I remembered hearing was *nausea, vomiting, hair loss, sores, possible sterility*—the list went on. But only one stuck in my mind, and that was *possible sterility. If I have this treatment, there may actually be a chance that I may never be able to conceive a child. Mike and I have always wanted to have two children together. How will we deal with this? Is it worth the chance?* "What will happen if I choose not to have the chemotherapy?" I asked the doctor.

"You most likely will end of having kidney failure and possibly death," the doctor responded.

"Okay, let's go ahead with the chemotherapy," I sadly replied.

I was also put on high-dose steroids, which unfortunately came with a long list of negative side effects as well. Doctors told me not to be surprised if I gained weight, had puffiness in my face, got acne, had mood swings, experienced depression—the list went on. All I could think about at this time was what I would look like walking down the aisle in my wedding dress.

I was also put on two different blood pressure medications and a proton-pump inhibitor to control gastroesophageal reflux disease.

I had a hole drilled into my chest in order for a catheter to be placed, making it easier to receive my plasmaphesis treatments. The most unbelievable part of this was that the day of this procedure was Saturday, May 16th, 1998, the original date of my dream wedding. As the doctor was drilling the hole into my chest just below my collarbone, I heard the sound of the famous game show *Jeopardy* coming from the television in my hospital room. "Lie very still," the doctor insisted as he made his final move. My eyes drifted to the clock. It was exactly 7:35 p.m., the same time I probably would have been cutting a piece of wedding cake with my new husband if my original wedding date was planned. Right then and there, as I heard the sound of the medical drill and smelled the rubbing alcohol on my chest, I thanked God that my dream wedding was over four months away.

CHAPTER 3:

LIFE FOREVER CHANGED

"Hi, Dad. I'm so glad you are here," I said in a lethargic manner, just waking up from a nap. My dad was sitting at the foot of my hospital bed, just watching me. I wondered what he was thinking. The chemotherapy and medications had really wiped me out.

"Just take it easy," he said quietly. Dad would come up in the evenings after work to visit, and I loved to have him there. My dad has always been a quiet-mannered man, and people respect him tremendously. I cherished every moment my dad would visit me in the hospital, because I always felt that certain security when he was there. "Mom said you were worried about the hospital bill?" Dad asked.

"Yes, Dad, I'm sorry this had to happen when it did," I replied.

"I was able to get you covered under COBRA insurance, so you have nothing to worry about except getting well!" Dad insisted.

"Thank you so much. That is the best news I have heard all day!" I happily answered. My dad always works things out. He always does what is best for his family. He thinks about others first and himself last. I adore my father; he'll always be my hero.

I became a little worried when my extended family and friends whom I had not seen in a long time came to visit. I did not want them to think that I would not be going home soon. I knew their intentions were good and they cared, but it did scare me a bit. Even I was not told when I would be going home.

The chemotherapy treatments in the hospital were not as bad as I had expected. Although they made me quite nauseous and tired, I never got too sick. I felt safe being in the hospital during the treatments because I knew I had very good care there. I had a great team of doctors and trusted each and every one of them. The nurses were fantastic and always made sure I was comfortable each day.

I have to admit, it was difficult remembering all of the details during my stay in the hospital. The majority of the time,

I was on pain medication, which made me very lethargic and sleepy. However, other than the plasmapheresis treatments, the other procedure I do recall going through was the kidney biopsy. During this process, the doctor actually takes a tool and goes into the kidney through the back and removes a tiny piece of the kidney. This is done with no anesthesia; however, the back area is somewhat numb. There was some discomfort, but more anxiety on my part.

The kidney biopsy was ordered to find out the stage of kidney disease and so the doctors could to decide the best choice of treatment. I ended up having diffuse proliferate lupus nephritis with nephritic syndrome. Doctors told me that my kidneys may never function at 100 percent again. I thought to myself, *Just as long as they are working, that's all I care about at this point.*

I was by myself in my hospital bed one afternoon, just staring out of the window, thinking of all the reasons why this happened to me, when out of nowhere, an elderly Catholic priest walked through the door. His presence brought an instant peace and calmness to the room, which words can't describe. He introduced himself and said that one of my family members requested he come by to give me the host. Just then, my mom entered the room, surprised and a bit concerned, of course. Once she determined the reasoning behind the visit, her nerves were calmed. He graciously gave me the body of Christ and, without hesitation, raised his hand over my sick body and sang the most miraculous blessing either one of us has ever heard! To this day, we have kept that memory to treasure forever. That moment, we experienced something that cannot be explained on paper. It was a "you had to be there" occurrence.

From this day on, I had no fears of my lupus. I knew that this disease was not going to get me down and that I was going to fight with all of my being. Even the days when the chemo made me sick and prednisone made me mean, I was not going to give up. I was given strength, the good Lord's strength's from above, to conquer this crazy, horrible, unpredictable, life-threatening disease!

Finally, there was good news from the doctors. My blood counts were back to normal after ten days of hospitalization, May 11th thru May 21st. The chemotherapy and medications were creating improvement in my overall health. I was discharged with several medications and instructions for chemotherapy visits and doctor appointments. Nurses gave me the medication side-effects pamphlets and warned me once more what to expect. "Yes, I know," I replied in a discouraged tone. "The steroids will make me gain weight and the chemotherapy may make me lose hair. Not a pretty picture for a new bride."

I was sent home with mixed feelings. I was so grateful that the pain was gone and it wasn't cancer. Yet at the same time, I'm going to be married in four months. *What will I look like? Will Mike still want to marry me? Will I be able to find a job? Will I even be able to work? Or will I be too sick?* Question after question boggled my mind. I still had unfinished wedding details to finish. That reminded me, I had already purchased my wedding dress. *Will it still fit? The steroids are going to make me gain weight. Do I need to start looking for a wig?* I thought I was under stress before. That was nothing. *This* was stress! Although I had to remember to stay positive, it was getting difficult.

So I went *into* the hospital young, successful, ready to conquer the world, and sicker than anyone could imagine! I came *out* of the hospital with systemic lupus erythematosus, lupus nephritis with secondary hypertension, gastroesophageal reflux disease prophylaxis, pleurisy, pericardial effusion, photosensitivity dermatitis, arthritis, Reynaud's, abdominal pain, a rheumatologist, a cardiologist, a nephrologist, a hematologist, and a list of medications, but I was still alive! And I was so thankful to have very educated doctors and nurses who were able to give me an accurate diagnosis in order to treat and manage this disease appropriately!

When I got home, I organized all my pills in a pill box, making sure not to miss one day. The chemotherapy treatments were scheduled. I followed through with each and every appointment, making sure to follow doctors' orders. I wanted to get healthy, even if that meant Mike's wife was going to be a bit overweight and bald. I knew he loved me because he was going to vow to love me in sickness and in health until death do us part.

I will forever remember the first night home. I was not able to take a shower due to the hole in my chest from the catheter. Only baths were allowed for a week. I was having a difficult time washing my hair in the sink by myself due to my joint pain in my hands. Along came my dad, my hero. He gave me a chair, took the shampoo, and washed my hair for me. My dad was washing my hair at twenty-three years old. Maybe I was emotional from all of the medications I was on or maybe it really was a true moment of father-daughter love, but a tear came streaming down my face.

Mike was great. He loved me the same as always, maybe even more so. When I told him about the side effects of the treatments, he told me he just wanted me to be healthy. He said he would be there for me through it all. "If God wants us to have children, we will. It is His call," Mike told me. This made me feel much better, and I was so fortunate to have found such a wonderful man to marry.

Going through the chemotherapy treatments became tough. The day of the treatments, I had no problems. I went through it on an outpatient basis early in the morning and was home by late afternoon. However, by late evening, I started feeling the effects. The nausea set in. I began having horrible stomach pains and, of course, fatigue. Great weekends for a newlywed couple ... lying in bed all weekend suffering with the side effects. I remember wondering at times which was worse, the disease or the effects of the treatments. I promised myself I would never do this again. But two months later, there I was, back at the clinic, with an IV in my arm, watching the poison flow in. Knowing it would eventually save my life was all I could count on. I had faith and trust in my doctors and knew God was on my side and with me through it all.

I sometimes go back in time and think about when I was lying on the floor with severe nausea from not drinking enough and my stomach was in knots. I remember thinking, I should give this pain up for my sins. Then I asked God, "What did I do that was so bad to deserve this much pain and suffering?" I never did find an answer to that question. But have reason to believe that everything in life happens for a reason beyond our control. I even tried to go back and concentrate on the priest's beautiful blessing upon me in the hospital room. But the pain was just so overbearing.

As the summer months passed by, my lupus symptoms gradually disappeared. The medications were working in my favor. And much to my surprise (and the doctors' as well), the chemotherapy only thinned out my hair—which was in my favor anyway, because I had always thought my hair was way too thick! And the steroids actually made me *lose* weight. As a matter of fact, I lost all of the weight I gained. I was down to 112 pounds. I was eating healthy and able to exercise.

I could actually put the final touches on the wedding of my dreams and have fun with it because I was finally feeling well for the first time in a very long time. I was excited, anxious, and nervous, but best of all … I was healthy. And that, by far, was the best feeling ever!

CHAPTER 4:

MY FUTURE BEGINS

September arrived, and the wedding countdown began. I had been sending my resume out to schools, and a week before the wedding, I received a phone call from the district in which I did my internship. The principal asked if I would like to interview for a school social work position on the day before my wedding. Of course I could not turn down the opportunity and accepted the interview.

Normally, I would be incredibly nervous during such an important interview, but I think my nerves had already had the best of me. I mean, I would be promising to spend the rest of my life with one person in about twenty-four hours; how could I be tense about answering some social work interview questions? I honestly felt it was the most relaxed interview I had ever experienced, and I had a good vibe about the school and the employees I met there.

Saturday, September 12th, 1998 finally arrived, and I married my college sweetheart. I was healthy and happy. We had a beautiful, sunny, September day, thanks to Mom and Dad and the good Lord above! Mike and I went to Chicago for three days for a honeymoon. We originally wanted to take a cruise, but since I couldn't be in the sun, and I had chemotherapy scheduled for the weekend after the wedding, we cancelled that plan.

The day we returned from our honeymoon, I received a call from the school I had interviewed at, and they offered me the school social work position. I excitedly accepted. I was on my way. Finally, life was coming back together again.

In November, Mike and I purchased our first new home together. We bought all new appliances, furniture, and accessories. I was still on medications and chemotherapy, but doing well. Luckily, I was able to plan my chemotherapy on Fridays so that I would only have to miss one day of work each month. The school district was very understanding about my circumstance. The chemotherapy made me nauseous for a couple days, so the weekends were spent in bed. Thankfully, I was back on my feet at work by the time Mondays came.

For the next two years, I was slowly tapered off of medications. I would still get headaches every now and then and feel fatigued, but I could work and enjoy life. I loved my job working as a school social worker. The greatest joy was to hear a student or parent come to me and thank me for helping them. I learned a lot those years—about others, as well as myself.

Mike and I really thought about having children after two years of marriage. We always wanted two children. By October 2000, my doctor cleared me of all medications and said we were safe to start trying to become pregnant if we wanted. I was really thinking that the chemotherapy may have caused sterility and always thought we may end up having to adopt, although I didn't want to go down that avenue unless there was reason to. I always tended to think way too far ahead.

One day in early November 2000, I started feeling a little nauseous and I knew right away that I was pregnant. I just had an inkling—a mother's instinct I guess one would say. I bought a pregnancy test, which turned out positive. I was ecstatic beyond belief! I showed it to Mike when he arrived home from work. He was cautiously optimistic and excited, but didn't fully believe it to be true because it had happened so soon. I told him I would make an appointment with my doctor for the next day.

The next day couldn't come soon enough for me. Dr. Lang happily walked into the room and congratulated me.

I was overjoyed with the confirmation! He set me up with an appointment with a high-risk obstetrician because of my medical condition.

Thankfully my parents were due to come to our home that evening. I told them the good news. They were excited and asked right away how I was feeling. "I am elated!" I responded joyfully. I called everyone I knew that night and informed each person that soon there would be a new addition to the family. Although most couples usually wait three months before announcing news like this, I had an intuition that this child was meant to be.

I began to read about the risks of pregnancy and lupus. Many times, pregnancy can cause lupus flares during or, more frequently, after childbirth. I became concerned but prayed every day and night and put this child's life in God's hands. I trusted that He would take care of us no matter what circumstances should arise. Just as I put God in control while I was in the hospital, I put Him in control of our child. Because after all, this child belonged to Him.

I was able to have an ultrasound each month, which was really great. During my pregnancy, I never felt better. I did gain more weight than I probably should have. I was informed that this was a lot of water weight. I was monitored very closely with this weight gain. However, not once did I get sick, aside from a little nausea here and there. I never had any problems with my lupus through the entire pregnancy, and it was smooth sailing all along. This child inside was a true blessing from above.

The day we had the ultrasound to find out the gender was especially thrilling. Mike and I did not have a preference; as long as our child was healthy, that was all we were concerned about all along. When the nurse told us we were going to be proud parents of a little boy, we were overjoyed! This was most important because lupus tends to be more common in women than men, so my son would be at a much less risk of getting lupus. Once again, we were thanking our lucky stars above.

Eight and a half months later, on June 21st, 2001, at 196 pounds (yes, that's right, I gained 84 pounds and it was only one child), I was induced. I gave birth to a beautiful baby boy weighing 7 pounds and 6 ounces, measuring 18 inches long, named Ryan Michael. I had no complications before, during, or after the birth. We were so blessed. For the first two days after Ryan was born, Mike and I did not sleep. All we could do was just stare at our little miracle child and thank God for him. I felt terrific, physically and emotionally. No lupus symptoms appeared as anticipated. We were all so thankful!

Mike and I decided I would take time off of work to take care of Ryan. I wanted to be the one to see his first steps, hear his first words, and potty train him. Thankfully, we were in a position where we were able to do this. My school social work position allowed me a two-year leave and would let me come back to my job.

Two years had gone by with no lupus symptoms, and I honestly believed that my lupus had disappeared because I had no problems for so long. Then came spring 2003. New symptoms appeared. Terrible joint pain began. My entire right hand was so red, sore, and inflamed that I could not move it. I knew immediately that lupus was back. And, unfortunately, lupus does not just disappear!

I called Dr. Lang, who sent me for blood tests. Sure enough, the results showed that my lupus was flaring. Along with joint pain, I was also experiencing stomach pains, fatigue, headaches, and swollen glands in my neck. My doctor sent me to a rheumatologist because of the severity of the joint pain. I was not impressed with this particular doctor. He gave me a pain killer and did not seem to take my complaints seriously. "You are only twenty-nine years old. It's not like you have rheumatoid arthritis," he said. Obviously, this doctor was used to working with the elderly population.

For two months, I was able to keep the pains under control the best I could with the medications, until they wore off. By June, I was calling Dr. Lang back again. Thank goodness my doctor was so graciously understanding. He again set me up with another rheumatologist, with whom I was much more impressed. By July, I was taking steroids and painkillers.

Needless to say, I did not return to work. Not because I didn't want to, but rather because my health would not allow me to. I could barely take care of my own family, much less work outside the home.

August and September passed by. Severe stomach cramps caused excruciating pains in my abdomen. My doctor scheduled an abdominal ultrasound to rule out a mass. The ultrasound came back clear. October blood work showed lupus was flaring and I had to increase steroid dosage. I was introduced to a new nephrologist (kidney specialist), Dr. Gratiot-Deans. She wasted no time and ordered blood work and a kidney biopsy immediately.

For the rest of 2003, into 2004, I was struggling with the same medications I was on back in 1998. The only difference was that my body was not reacting the same positive way. My lupus was not getting under control. If anything, it was getting worse, and no one knew why. I was trying my best to be a good mom to Ryan, who was now two years old. I slept every minute he slept; thankfully, he still took afternoon naps! My parents would come over to take care of Ryan whenever I needed them. They were so generous, and I don't know what I would have done without them. Mike would leave work on several occasions when my pains got the best of me. I was so worried he would lose his job.

It was March 2004. I had been suffering from horrible migraine headaches, fatigue, and generalized aches and pains. Since it was a weekend, I made a visit to the medical center because the pain was out of control. There, I received a pain injection, which helped temporarily. The next Monday, I had an appointment with Dr. Gratiot-Deans, who sent me to the hospital for tests. There doctors performed a magnetic resonance imaging (MRI) of my head. Results showed two small lesions on the brain. Further follow up was necessary. I stayed overnight in the hospital and was sent home on high-dose steroids, medication for my migraines, and Cellcept for the lupus.

One day while I watched Ryan nap peacefully, I sat and cried because I knew what the possible effects of the medications were. I knew it would be much more difficult this time because now I had a child here who needed me. A beautiful, energetic two-year-old child who was used to having his happy-go-lucky mommy home every day. I felt this wasn't fair to him. This particular lupus flare caused severe emotional reactions I have never had to deal with before, and I wasn't quite sure how to handle them. I didn't feel like an adequate mother, wife, or human being whatsoever. I felt myself sinking into deep depression.

Thankfully, my mother encouraged me to keep a journal of my medical reports from the very beginning. Along with this, I would write to my son when I felt the need to do so, at the lowest times of my depression.

March 22nd, 2004: Dear Ryan, Mommy has been really sick lately—a lupus flare. I pray to God you do not get this horrible disease! Yes, it could be worse, but being sick has caused me to miss out on fun things with you. Mom and Dad were supposed to bring you to the circus, but my chemotherapy has made me so sick that I had to stay home, so Daddy took you himself. You had fun, but Mom wanted to be there so badly! This is so hard because I want to be healthy so I can take good care of you, but not only does lupus make me so sick, so do the treatments! I'm not sure which is worse. It is a no-win situation. I'm so lucky that you have such a great daddy and you love him so much. He has been such a great help recently. So have Grandma and Grandpa. We are so fortunate to have such a wonderful, loving, supportive family!

Ryan, I just want to say this: if I do die before you understand all of this, please know that all I ever wanted in life was to be your mommy and love you and watch you grow, learn, love, and laugh. I pray that we will always know and love each other no matter want happens. God loves you and loves me and will make sure the love between us never dies, even if you don't remember me.

I love you so much, Ryan; don't forget that! You are wonderful!

Love, Mommy

I was at my lowest. I almost did not want to stop writing that journal entry. But then the joint pain in my fingers reminded me why I had to put my pen down and the reason I was taking the annoying medications in the first place! Not only did I feel as though I was physically going to die, but at times, when pain was the greatest, I prayed to God that He would just silently end the pain for me in my sleep.

I did not want to admit to anyone how great this depression was. I felt I would appear weak. Not talking to someone probably caused my depression to become worse.

I did have a follow-up appointment with my physician where the topic of depression briefly came up during our discussion when talking about my symptoms. By this point, my physician knew me well and could tell depression may be an issue for me. I denied any significant problems that may need medication or counseling. Even the thought of counseling, which was brought up during our conversation, mortified me. After all, this was what I went to college for—to learn how to help other people with their problems. And here I was, after six years of hard work, considering admitting that I needed help myself. No, it was not going to happen, not on my watch. I refused any professional help. This was a mistake.

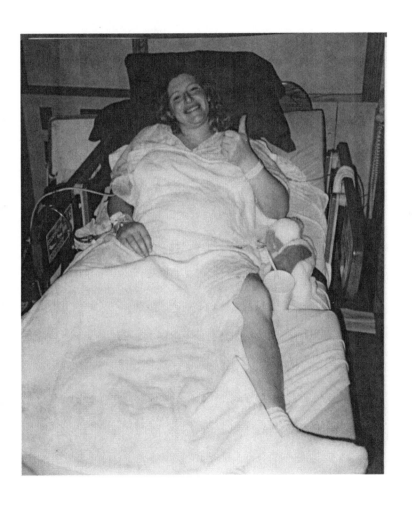

CHAPTER 5:

SO THIS IS PAIN?

It was March 23rd, 2004, and my health kept going downhill. I wanted the most to pray to God to just take the pain from me. However, I didn't even have the energy to pray—I was that sick. My stomach pains became so severe. I remember lying on the floor playing with Ryan; I literally had to crawl to the phone to call Mike at work to tell him to come home and bring me to the hospital. I felt like a regular there; they knew me by name—kind of sad. The doctor did a CAT scan of the stomach, which showed inflammation and a urinary tract infection. Also, I had an ultrasound and colonoscopy, which came back normal. I was discharged on March 26th.

I was woken up on March 28th by horrible chest pains and shortness of breath. I knew once again I desperately needed medical attention but was very hesitant to go back to the hospital. I could imagine what the doctors must be thinking of me. "Oh, her again!" I couldn't blame them. But the pain was so real and hurt so bad, I didn't know what else to do. My mom came over to my house and insisted she take me to the emergency room. I'm so glad she insisted. I stayed in the hospital for four days in order to just get the pain under control. *My poor Ryan, he probably thinks his mother has abandoned him. I don't feel like I have been there for him the way a mother should.*

Journal entry: Friday, April 9th, 2004

My mom was telling me today that when I was in the hospital with my stomach pains, the gastroenterologist told her that I needed an anti-depressant because he couldn't find anything wrong with me. I have lupus! *Oh yeah, it must be all in my head. The anxiety is making me sick; better give me more meds so I stop complaining! I almost wish he would have found something that was causing the pain so he knew I was telling the truth! The pain is real! I do not need medication! If I hear it is all in my head again, I will become depressed and will need medication.*

Sunshine is my enemy. My son loves to play outside. I have to wear sunscreen each and every time I am exposed to the sun, even for short periods. Some lupus patients have a sensitivity to the sun, which can cause a rash. I am always sure to limit my time outside. This was sometimes difficult when Ryan would see the other kids playing and I would have to tell him that we had enough time outside today. He was too young to understand why this rule existed. Eventually, he adjusted and did not ask questions. Even today, I tell him that too much sun is not good for anyone and we have to limit our exposure. He is very appreciative of this rule.

It was late afternoon when the joints in my hand became extremely inflamed and sore to the touch. I could not even bend my fingers without wincing in pain. The throbbing was so intense, I couldn't wait until Monday. I thought to myself that I was having a really bad month this time around with gaining extra water weight. So I decided to take some pills to help with that. I immediately took two water retention pills to see if that would help, along with some Tylenol for the pain. Not only did it not help, but I felt worse! I figured two pills were not strong enough for me and went ahead and took two more of each. The pain continued to get more severe until I could not bear it any longer. At this point, I knew it was more than the monthly symptoms I normally experienced. This was not something I had dealt with during a flare before; these were different symptoms. In my mind, I knew my lupus was flaring, but did not want to believe it was true. Lupus flares can present different symptoms. I was scared. I literally could not use my right hand at all.

Since my mom was over watching my son, she encouraged me to go to the medical center, since the doctor's office was closed for the day. Without hesitation, I drove myself, with my left hand. Thankfully, I had an automatic, not a stick shift vehicle, which would have made it much more difficult. Although the medical center was only ten minutes away, it felt like it took me three hours to get there.

Luckily, I was able to get in right away. The doctor took an X-ray of my hand, telling me I had no broken bones. Well, I could have told him that. I guess by the looks of my swollen hand, one would assume my hand was broken. I was given a steroid shot to reduce the swelling. Yet I wanted pain relief in the worst way. I came to find out that doctors like to wait until they know what is really going on before they just hand out the pain medication, which, to a point, I can understand, but I have lupus! And I as in *pain!* I had an extensive chart, and I was not there for fun, and I was definitely *not* a drug addict. But I guess the doctor was just doing his job. Eventually, I did receive pain medication after he reviewed my chart thoroughly. Later that week, I went to my primary physician. He started me back on low-dose steroids and did blood work to check kidney function.

I met with my nephrologist, who called for a kidney biopsy. The biopsy showed stage 3 focal proliferation. I was put back on 60 mg of prednisone and Cellcept. The blood tests were not improving ,and my symptoms were not disappearing. I had fatigue, joint pain, and headaches, and the last CAT scan and MRI showed two lesions on the back of my brain. The only positive thing was that Ryan was still taking naps every day, so I could sleep in the afternoon when he did. On several occasions, I had to call Mike or my mom home from work to take care of Ryan because my pain was so great.

March 16th, 2004, was the day I possibly had the worst migraine headache ever! After six hours of excruciating pain and vomiting, I could not take it any longer. My mom called an ambulance to our house. As the medical personnel made their way into the bathroom, all I could do was pray that Ryan would not wake up from his nap and have to see his mother go through this. I was taken to the hospital via ambulance, where I continued to be sick. I was given anti-nausea and pain medication and sent home.

Three days later, I underwent Cytoxan chemotherapy. My chemo usually made me slightly nauseous, but the worst part was that it gave me terrible stomach pains. *I see this poison going into my body and I know it is doing good things for me, yet I know it is going to make me sick at the same time. It feels like a no-win situation. I am told by the nurses to drink lots of fluids in order for the chemo to flush through my body. I try so hard to do just that.*

However, I am feeling horrible. I am nauseous and my stomach hurts; the last thing I want to do is drink, drink, drink. Yet I know it is the best thing for me. I feel separate from my body.

April 2ⁿᵈ, 2004, Dr. Gratiot-Deans recommended she make an appointment at the Mayo Clinic in Rochester, Minnesota. Some of the newest treatments and medications are developed by doctors known world-wide. Hesitant but eager, I agreed to the plan. My trip was scheduled for June 2004. My mom planned on taking the hour-and-a-half plane trip with me. I would spend the week there for tests, hoping for a treatment plan to put me back into a remission again (little did I know that this trip might be the trip that saved my life).

Waiting for that appointment for two and a half months felt like a lifetime. The days just dragged on. I was so thankful to have such wonderful family support. Mike was taking such great care of not just me but our son, as well. I could not have asked for a better father for Ryan. My husband Mike was always, and still is, so understanding of my disease and took every part of it so seriously.

My parents have also been so great in taking care of me and my family since the beginning of my diagnosis. Any time I call on them for help, day or night, they are there to help in any way. *God has blessed me in many ways. I may have lupus, but looking back now, I see it as a blessing. And as the saying goes, "I have lupus, but lupus doesn't have me!"*

As the weeks passed, I continued to take my pain relievers to get me by until the trip, which did little good. I got rest when I could but still felt absolutely horrible and knew that the trip would come just in time. My son would be turning three years old towards the end of June, so I hoped I would be well for his birthday after the trip.

•

CHAPTER 6:

MAYO CLINIC STAY

Finally, the day was here. We arrived at the Mayo Clinic on June 7th with high expectations. We stayed at the hotel directly across from the Mayo Clinic. This made it accessible so I could get to my appointments easily and arrive on time. I was given somewhat of a medical itinerary for each day of my stay. All five days were filled back-to-back with blood tests, chest X-rays, head MRIs, CAT scans, doctor visits and, yes, more blood tests! I met with the top-notch rheumatologists, nephrologists, and neurologists in the country in hopes of finding a treatment that would put my lupus back into remission.

I can remember one of the nights lying in the hotel room like it was yesterday. My pain was so intense that my body felt separate from my soul. Maybe on a subconscious level, I was trying to disconnect myself from what was going on with my body. All I know is that I recognized what it felt like to hit rock bottom. I was by far the sickest I had ever been in my entire life at that very moment in time. I prayed. I thanked God that my son was not there watching his mom go through this!

As each result from the tests came back, it was as I knew all along: my kidneys were slowly failing and the blood tests were not looking good—all due to my lupus. By the final day, I was ready to leave. I was completely overwhelmed, exhausted, and sick, and most of all, I missed my family more than ever. This was the longest time I had ever been away from Ryan.

Finally, the last appointment arrived, just a few hours before I was to get back on the plane and go back home. As I walked in, the nurse informed me that the nephrologist was running a little late. She took my vitals and seemed a bit concerned. My blood pressure was quite high and I had a fever. When I questioned her about it, I could tell she did not want me to worry, and she told me it could be due to caffeine or anxiety. (Gee, haven't heard that before.) The nurse had me wait in the examination room, and she paged the doctor, more than once. I became quite uneasy. Twenty minutes went by—no doctor. She paged him again; another twenty minutes, no doctor. I became frustrated and decided to leave. After all, I was sick and tired of being sick and tired and just wanted to go home. I told the nurse I did not want to miss my flight back home. She looked troubled but knew it was my decision and apologized.

Honestly, I was afraid if I did not take the chance to get up and leave then, I might have ended up staying there a lot longer than originally planned.

There was a message waiting for me on my answering machine as soon as I walked in the door to my house. It was from the last doctor I was to meet with. He kindly apologized for the inconvenience (he had emergency surgery). He read my chart and came up with a treatment plan for me, which I felt possibly saved my life!

This doctor, the nephrologist from the Mayo Clinic, discussed that his treatment of choice would be for my doctor to administer an IV chemo treatment called Rituxan, a new treatment option for lupus nephritis patients, in conjunction with Cytoxan. This would treat my lupus symptoms, including the nephritis. Rituxan is a treatment traditionally used for non-Hodgkin's lymphoma patients. It was most recently considered as an experimental treatment for lupus nephritis patients. This treatment of choice has only been used with a handful of lupus patients worldwide and may be a risky choice. The long-term effects have not been studied, and this treatment is not guaranteed to be successful.

I decided to take the risk. It was my only choice at this point in the game. I respected the doctors at the Mayo Clinic, and my doctor would not have sent me there if she did not trust their opinions as well.

I was so happy to arrive home to see my family. It seemed like I felt better just seeing them. Later that week, after arriving back home, I talked to my doctor, and we planned the treatment immediately. My doctor seemed cautiously optimistic, and I felt the same. Just knowing that so few lupus patients had used this treatment, and realizing the long-term ramifications were unknown at this point, made me a bit apprehensive. But did I have to lose? Mike, my mom, and the rest of my family just wanted me to get better, so we just had to take whatever option we had. Considering that was the last option, there was really no choice in the matter. We all believed in the power of prayer, as well, so we all said a prayer and hoped everything would turn out for the best. By this point, I was so sick that I would do anything to feel better.

CHAPTER 7:

REMISSION FOR LIFE?

Thankfully, I was able to get through my son's third birthday. My doctor requested I be in the hospital at this time, but I compromised and was able to do an outpatient treatment of IV steroids the day before just to get me through the birthday party. A mother will do anything for her child, regardless of her own needs.

June 23, 2004 was my first Rituxan/Cytoxan treatment, exactly two days after Ryan turned three years old. Everything went well. There were no problems during the treatment. However, the following day, I felt excruciating pain in both legs, like I'd never felt before. My doctor said it wasn't a common side effect, but it sure was real to me. She suggested I go back to the hospital. There, I was given a morphine drip, which I controlled. The pain was so bad that the medication did not even give relief. I ended up getting sick from the morphine.

I received different pain medication, and by the next day, the pain subsided.

The second drawback from the treatment was the anemia I developed. I was at home and became extremely dizzy and had terrible chest pains. I yet again called my doctor. She encouraged me to go to the emergency room as soon as possible. I was hesitant due to the fact I was just there. I did not want to appear to be or be labeled as a hypochondriac. I told her I was going to just wait it out a while before I went. She said that would be a bad idea and persuaded me to get there before waiting any longer. I thankfully decided to take her professional recommendation and went to the hospital. My red blood cell count was severely low. I ended up receiving a blood transfusion and stayed one night for observation.

I felt better by the next day and had no further problems. My lupus symptoms remained under control and seemed to be gradually subsiding as time went on. The second Rituxan/Cytoxan treatment was a month later. This time it was uneventful. I was in and out of the hospital within eight hours, with no side effects. This was good news for both me and my family.

My disease has improved since the Rituxan treatments. I still have my good and bad days. But this is expected with a disease such as lupus. My fatigue never improved much, but I can't complain considering everything I went through. As for the migraines, I have been prescribed new medication to prevent the frequency of the onset of them. In the end, this treatment was the best treatment for me.

In October 2005, I developed a terrible cold and cough which lasted for three months. This was possibly due to the fact that I was on steroids for so long, which suppresses the immune system. My cold was so bad that I would just lie in bed most days from the fatigue. By early December, I was coughing so hard that doctors thought that may be what caused me to break three ribs on my right side. X-rays also showed a nodule on my lung, which has not changed and needs to continuously be monitored. Breaking ribs is so painful because there is no way to heal these broken bones except time. I literally could not stand up straight or walk well. It hurt tremendously to even breathe. I ended up going to a pain clinic, where they gave me Fentanyl patches until the ribs healed. This controlled the pain. I was slowly weaned off the patches. Thankfully, I did not have to stay on the patches for long. The side effects included severe fatigue, and I would wake up in the middle of the night with horrifying nightmares.

I was continuing to have awful intermittent stomach pains, which I'd had in the past. I had CAT scans, ultrasounds, and a colonoscopy, and doctors found nothing. They thought it may just be simple inflammation of the stomach lining. Wow, how can something so simple hurt so much? No pain medication helped with this terrible pain, so the doctor prescribed muscle relaxers, which took the edge off, at least. The fatigue did not seem to subside at all. The medication I continue to take to control the migraines and depression may play a part in causing the fatigue. I have to take the medication. I really think if I had the chance, I could sleep all day and all night. This may be chronic fatigue, as well.

Since I was a little girl, I have always been a planner. I looked back at my high school journal where it asked where you want to be in twenty years. I wrote that I would be working as a school teacher and happily married, with two children. Oh, so close! I'm not working, have one beautiful, healthy child, and I am happily married. My mom always tells me, "You make plans, and God laughs." She's right. God had other plans for me. I feel God chose me to make a positive difference in the lives of others by bringing awareness to the disease lupus. Although our original plan was to have two children, Mike and I chose not to bring another child into this world. I am so afraid that it would be unfair to. I am fatigued so often, which requires much-needed rest. I get migraines, have intense stomach pains, and never know when the next lupus flare may come. How in the world would I be able to take care of another child? I dreaded having to be in the hospital as often as I was when Ryan was so young. To have to relive that frightens me more than ever! I don't feel healthy enough, and doctors agree it would not be the best decision for me.

Journal entry, July 2006: Dear Ryan, Mommy wants to write you something very special. Mom and Dad have decided to have you be our one and only sweet and special child—our blessing from God. For my own health and the benefit of you and our family, we feel this is the best choice. I could get very sick again, and I don't want it to affect anyone negatively in any way. I love you too much! I really hope you understand this and are not too upset about being an only child. I'm sure you'll be fine. You are such a happy child. You have wonderful cousins who love you tremendously and treat you like a brother, and you make friends wherever you go. I love you, Ryan!

Love, Mommy

In some strange way, by writing in my journal, it felt as though I was telling Ryan what I wanted him to know. There have been occasions where he questioned why he doesn't have a playmate at home. I told him I just wanted *him* to love. Now he may be old enough to be told the truth, but I may be brought to tears. I'm longing for the day he will be able to read this book. I allow Ryan to have friends come over to play often, and he goes to friends' houses regularly as well, because he yearns for playtime with children as much as the next child. We live in a wonderful family-oriented neighborhood, where the neighbors are willing to lend support to one another at any time. Many neighborhood activities and events are planned throughout the year, so Ryan really has no reason to complain about having no one around. He has more than enough playmates right outside his own door!

CHAPTER 8:

LIFE GOES ON...

God does work in mysterious ways! I will believe that until the day I am lucky enough to meet my creator. My twenty-two-year-old brother-in-law, Luke, came to live with us in September of 2007, while going to college. Ryan and Luke get along very well and have a good time together playing video games, working on homework, and reading books with each other. It didn't take long for Ryan to refer to Luke as his big brother. Although I get some looks from people when Ryan tells others that he has a twenty-two-year-old brother, Ryan loves the fact that Luke is part of the family and is always there for him when he needs someone other than Mom or Dad to go to.

My family—second to God, of course—has been top priority in my life; always has been, always will be. Without them, I would not be the person I am today. We have a very close extended family, which, much to my surprise, I found out is pretty rare these days. My mom and dad have been my ultimate saviors in helping care for our son when Mike had to take me to the hospital or care for me when I was too sick to care for myself. I am so thankful to have an amazing sister who has rushed over at the drop of a hat to take care of my son when she heard I was too ill to get out of bed. My wonderful aunts would be there in a heartbeat if they knew I was in pain and needed help at any time. And, of course, Luke, a blessing in disguise, many times has come home to find me lying on the couch, fatigued. He always entertained Ryan until Mike came home from work.

If I were to walk by on the street, people might look at me and think to themselves, "She has it all together." Boy, would they be wrong. Lupus is such a hidden disease. I have so many symptoms that the eye cannot see. Some days are good; some days are bad. It is very frustrating! Probably the most frustrating part about having lupus for me is when I have a day where I feel horrible. I will have a headache, joint pain, and fatigue, and someone will say to me, "Wow, you sure are looking good today!" But I have to say, I have been very lucky in life. My graduation, wedding, job, childbirth, and all the important events in my life seemed to fall into place at just the right time. I have to thank God for giving me lupus because He has given me the chance to write this book to reach out to others to give them the awareness of this very real, yet unpredictable, hidden disease.

Today, my son Ryan is seven years old and does not know about my disease. I think someday I will explain it all to him. But he is too young to understand everything and much too sensitive a child to have to worry. What Ryan does know is that his mom gets sick a lot. Many times, he sees me suffering from migraines and is the most compassionate child I've seen. "Mom," he'll say in a caring voice, "you lie your head down on this pillow while I go get you an ice pack for your head. Do you want a juice box?" He is always concerned when I am sick. He has watched me suffer with aches and pains more than a seven-year-old should have to watch his mother suffer.

Ryan once decided to come up with his own concoction to cure headaches. He went to his bathroom sink and mixed some of his toothpaste, mouthwash, and hair gel together in a little Dixie cup. He took a cotton swap and dabbed the mixture across my forehead and told me this would take away my pain in ten minutes. If only life were that simple!

That day, Ryan looked up at me and says, "Mom, when I grow up, I want to be a doctor, so when you are sick, I can take away all of your pain and you won't want to sleep so much during the day." It took so much to keep the tears from coming down my face.

I struggle with the idea of ever having to explain lupus to my son. I read in books that honesty is the best policy, that children should learn as much about your condition as they can understand. It makes so much sense that my child should understand why I may not have the energy to do certain things one day or be really tired the next. I just really hate the idea of having to worry my child over something not worth worrying about.

Every couple months, I get blood work drawn to check on my lupus. One day, I took Ryan with me, and he asked me why I had to "get a shot" so often. I answered him by saying my doctor wanted to be sure I stay healthy. He looked at me with inquisitive eyes and responded with the question, "Why doesn't *everybody* get a shot as much as you do?" That was it; I was busted! My own seven-year-old can outwit me. I do not remember my reply to this question. I think I must have changed the subject.

For the past three years, my mom, husband, and I have attended the annual lupus walk. However, the year 2006 had much more of an impact on me than the past years. This was because of the fact that we met so many people who had many stories to tell of their very similar pains, both physical and emotional, which I could relate to in every way. Little did I realize just how many people suffered from this same disease and lived in such close proximity to each other.

When I attend the lupus walks every year, I am reminded of how fortunate I am. I continue to see other people in wheelchairs who have been affected by lupus. I hear others stories about how they also struggle day to day with the brutal symptoms of lupus. Some who attend the walk do so because they think they may have lupus but have not yet been diagnosed. I can imagine how much pain they must be going through. These individuals do not yet even have medications or treatments to control their symptoms.

My mom had always tried to encourage me to attend the lupus support groups in town. However, I was too much of a coward to go. I imagined the meetings where everyone sits in a circle feeling sorry for themselves, crying away their sorrows. I figured all they did was come up with ways to live with lupus when you have no energy, no contentment, or no intimacy. Nonetheless, I met a lady who changed my view on this. She mentioned to me that these meetings could be extremely beneficial to me. I could learn a great deal of pertinent information, which would be very helpful. New medications, treatments, and ways to manage the symptoms of lupus were discussed and exchanged among the participants. This is very useful for others who are looking for support. I never looked at it that way. I could be so much of a support to others with my very own story. This precise conversation encouraged me to continue writing my book. I want others to hear and listen to what I have been through and to know that they are not alone, because several times, I felt so very alone, especially at the beginning when I was extremely sick. I did not want to tell anyone how sick I was because they would worry. When I did tell the experts how sick I was, I wasn't even believed! One of these days, I may attend a lupus support group.

My brother-in-law, Luke, who currently is living with us, introduced me to MySpace. I originally thought of this internet craze as a younger generation trend. However, as I created my own profile, I realized that I could connect with other individuals who also suffered with the same difficulties in having lupus. I felt much more comfortable talking with others without having to sit down together in a group setting. I now belong to a group online called Butterflies among Us. Here we can talk about the real feelings we have and know that we are not alone. We help each other out and offer advice to one another. I've made many friends through this group. They have become my second family!

One of my MySpace friends, Sondra Hildreth, wrote an awesome blog on her site. She had a lupus resolution called *Make the Wolf Pay!* This is what it said:

I resolve that for every second of pain, fatigue, exhaustion, illness, and infection, *I will make the wolf pay!*

For every moment of confusion and incomprehension because of brain fog, *I will make the wolf pay!*

For every night without sleep, every day with fever, every migraine, every time I can't have anything and, more important, anyone touch my skin because the nerves are hyper-sensitive, *I will make the wolf pay!*

For every time I have to watch everyone else enjoy the sunlight while I stay in the shade, for every hive, rash, and week of exhaustion from one hour in the sun, *I will make the wolf pay!*

For every time my parents look at me and worry that their youngest child will die before them, for every tear my mother cries, for every time my father worries about me and has to console my mother while silently consoling himself, *I will make the wolf pay!*

For every moment of depression, doubt, or envy towards those who don't battle this wolf, *I will make the wolf pay!*

For every day that my eyes are affected, every time my hearing falters, every step that hurts, every handshake that leaves me shaking, *I will make the wolf pay!*

For every day of my life I miss because I'm too sick to leave bed, every time I need assistance going from room to room, every time I have to lean on a wall so I don't fall down, every time I have to say I'm fine when I wish I were in bed dying because no one wants to hear how I really am, *I will make the wolf pay!*

For every step closer I come to having crippled hands and the possibility of blindness, for every time lab tests come back with worrisome results concerning my organs, *I will make the wolf pay!*

For every day I have to wake up and realize I'm too disabled to work yet struggling to have the government agree with my doctors about that, for every second of frustration because of that, *I will make the wolf pay!*

I will fight to live my life. I will not go down easily. I will not surrender. I will take my meds and risk the side effects and possible medical damage in the future so that I may live more comfortably with my family and loved ones in the present. I will chose a shorter but happier and more fulfilling life with those I love rather than a longer life where I'm too sick and sore to enjoy it. I will be happy with the time I have and strive to make it worth more. I will not surrender anything to this disease without a fight. *I refuse to just roll over and die!*

I will draw my pictures despite the fact that my hands will be crippled for the next two days when I'm done. I will use my sculpting tools and create beautiful things even though you are determined to leave my hands shaped like claws. I will laugh at myself when I misunderstand things or when my words get tangled because of the fog you put in my brain. I will spend those days in bed but make sure I thoroughly enjoy the days when you can't pin me to my room. I will spend time with my friends, laugh with my family, hug and play with my nieces and nephews.

For everything taken from me, *I will make the wolf pay dearly!*

Do you hear me, wolf? I know you're here and I know you're listening! I won't go down easily! I will fight you to the last breath! Look out, wolf, because I've taken your challenge and I intend to be the winner!

When I read this blog by Sondra, I was in awe! I had to contact her and tell her how much I appreciated the way she described how she felt about this very horrible, unpredictable disease. I could relate to her emotions regarding lupus.

Right from the start, people have been misled by lupus. According to *Living with Lupus* by Mark Horowitz and Marietta Brill, an early sign of this deception is seen in the name: *lupus* means "wolf" in Latin. It was first coined by a doctor in the thirteenth century to describe the skin marks sometimes seen in people with lupus. These lesions were similar to and might have been mistaken for the bite of a wolf. However, lupus has nothing to do with a wolf bite. But the name is oddly appropriate.

CHAPTER 9:

WE NEED A CURE!

At the present time, I am not working. I honestly don't see how I could. I desperately need my eight hours of sleep each night and an afternoon nap due to my chronic fatigue. I truly doubt many schools would allow a social worker a daily afternoon nap each day. Migraines tend to attack unexpectedly, causing me to be bed-ridden immediately, not to mention the medication I take for the migraines causes drowsiness and dizziness. I have cold sweats at night and some chest pains, and the stomach pains are an ongoing problem for me. I'm not sure any employer would keep me around for long.

My mom encouraged me to apply for disability, knowing how often I get sick and how many times she and my husband left work because of my illness. I even had a doctor bring up the issue in conversation at one point. I researched the requirements for disability and decided to apply. The information I read basically said that the first application is usually always denied, but to keep trying and not to give up. I expected this was what I would be in store for. It was a lengthy, time-consuming process, but worth the wait. Much to my surprise, I was considered disabled by the Social Security administration the first time. Of course, the money is not nearly close to what I would be making with a master's degree in social work, and I would much rather be out there doing what I worked so hard to do and what I love best. However, I just can't physically work right now.

I am a member of the National Lupus Foundation and receive every newspaper, pamphlet, and magazine on lupus out there. I want to know the latest treatments, medications, and therapies for lupus. I sometimes feel as though I could teach a class on lupus, I know so much. After I was diagnosed, I went to every book store in town and bought every paperback on lupus I could find. I researched every article on the internet and printed every story I read. The downside is that lupus is such a complex disease and it affects every person differently. It is an extremely complicated disease that can perplex even the most educated doctors. My husband Mike and I are pushing for lupus to get the attention that it needs. Mike continues to contact the National Lupus Foundation and donates when he can.

One important thing I did learn at a young age is that you know your own body and you know when something is not right. Keep fighting for yourself until you are satisfied with the results. Save records of all tests, treatments, and procedures. Write a journal of all doctor appointments and lab tests, and document all of the sick days and be specific. Thankfully, I have a great family physician and nephrologist on my side. Family and friends' prayers got me through a lot of difficult times—what a blessing!

In October of 2006, I had my fifteen-year high school class reunion. Many people did not recognize me—not because the lupus symptoms changed my looks, but because my hair was short and highlighted. When I tell others of my disease, they truly have a difficult time believing I could *be* or could *have been* so sick. The lupus I suffer from is internal, systemic, and very painful, hidden and unpredictable. I can be feeling great at nine o' clock in the morning and not so great at noon. I just don't know from day to day or hour to hour.

I have to continue to remind myself daily that I could have it ten times worse. I pray and give thanks to God that He has blessed me with lupus. As strange as that might sound, that is how I see it. I was given the chance to live life with lupus, good or bad. I feel it has helped me become a better individual overall. I am writing to express my emotions so others can relate and know that the feelings are real and not be ashamed of doing or saying what they believe is right. I also continue to pray for everyone that someday, very soon, there will indeed be a cure for lupus, fibromyalgia, and all diseases!

A FEW FACTS ABOUT LUPUS

What Is Lupus?

Lupus is an autoimmune disease. The immune system, which normally protects the body, turns against itself and attacks it. Lupus has no known cause and, as of yet, no cure. Lupus is not contagious. It is more common in women in their child-bearing years than men. The disease can affect many different systems of the body, and there are many different ways that it can affect people. The three types of lupus are systemic, discoid, and drug-induced, with systemic being the most life-threatening.

Eleven Criteria for the Diagnosis of Lupus:

1. Rash across the face: redness or rash across the face may appear in a butterfly configuration on the malar ridge or cheeks.

2. Discoid rash: a rash that can involve blotches or raised, scaly lesions.

3. Sun-sensitivity: a harmful physiological reaction to sunlight that is more severe than just a sunburn.

4. Ulcers in the mouth or nose: frequent development of these sores may indicate lupus.

5. Inflammation of joints: Arthritic inflammation or pain in two or more joints can be a criterion of lupus. Joint problems can show up as swelling, tenderness, or pain if the joint is moved.

6. Inflammation of the lining of the lungs or heart: this is called pleurisy in the lungs and pericarditis in the heart.

7. Kidney disorder: excessive protein in the urine (proteinuria), existence of cell casts. Casts are fragments of cells normally found in the blood or fragments of the tubules of the kidney itself. If kidney disease exists, various casts may be found in the urine.

8. Nervous system disorder: convulsions (seizures) or psychotic behavior can also be caused by drugs or a metabolic

dysfunction. When this is not the case, this is a criterion for lupus.

9. Blood system disorder: this involves particular changes in the blood. Hemolytic anemia: red blood cells are coated with antibodies that cause them to break down and break apart. Leukopenia: a low white blood cell count. Lymphopenia: a decrease in the number of lymphocytes in the blood. Thrombocytopenia: low numbers of platelets in the blood.

10. Immune disorder: presence of the LE cell (a lupus erythematosus cell contains two nuclei rather than the one nucleus that cells usually have) and a false positive reaction to the test for syphilis.

11. A *positive* ANA: the body's production of *antinuclear antibodies* (antibodies that work against cell nuclei) is the final criterion for the diagnosis of lupus.

By consensus of experts, at least four of the eleven criteria should be present before a diagnosis of lupus is made.

The most commonly used tests in the diagnosis of lupus are the ANA, anti-DNA, anticardiolipin, and the anti-Smith (Sm) blood tests.

Symptoms of Lupus:

- **General symptoms: weakness, fatigue, low-grade fevers, generalized aching, and chills.**

- Skin: rashes, patchy lesions, red inflammations. Scarring on the scalp may cause hair loss.

- Chest: chest pain due to pleurisy or pericarditis, causing difficulty breathing, pain, shortness of breath, and rapid heartbeat. Inflammation of the rib area or in the abdominal muscles may cause chest pain as well.

- Muscular system: weakness, aches, and pains.

- Joints: arthritis-like pain, swelling, redness, and stiffness.

- Blood: low red blood cell count (anemia), decreased white blood cell count (leading to chance of infection).

- Cardiac or circulatory system: increased swelling of the extremities, accumulation of fluid in the sac surrounding the heart, and Raynaud's phenomenon.

- Digestive system: stomach pain, cramps, nausea, vomiting, diarrhea, and constipation.

- Kidneys: decreased kidney functioning, leading to *uremia* (increased waste products remaining in circulation), proteinuria (excessive protein lost in the urine).

- Nervous system: headaches, seizures, temporary paralysis, psychotic behavior, or stoke.

Treatment of Lupus:

Treatment varies depending on the individual and the severity of the lupus symptoms.

Some medication and treatment options include the following:

- Plamapheresis

- Physical therapy

- Non-steroidal anti-inflammatory drugs

- Antimalarials

- Corticosteroids

- Pulse-therapy

- Immunosuppressive drugs (chemotherapy)

- Over-the-counter drugs

- Herbal remedies

- Exercise and diet

SOME HELPFUL LUPUS WEB SITES

http://www.lupus.org
http://www.lupus-support.org.uk
http://www.cerebel.com/lupus
http://www.mtio.com/lupus
http://www.healingwell.com/lupus/
http://www.lupusden.com
http://www.curezone.com/diseases/lupus

Feel free to visit my Web site at: myspace.com/ wwwmyspacecombabysteps

Also, for a great Web site to share experiences and for lupus support visit: http://www.lupus/fibromyal giabutterfliesamongus.com

REFERENCES

Horowitz, Mark, MD, and Marietta Brill Abrams. *Living with Lupus.* New York: Lowenstein Associates, 1994.

Lahita, Robert G., MD, and Phillips Robert, PhD. *Lupus: Everything You Need to Know.* New York: Avery Publishing Group, 1998.

Breinigsville, PA USA
10 November 2010
249130BV00001B/20/P